Let's chat

SIMPLE STEPS TO

SPEAK IN SPLENDID ENGLISH

(A HAND BOOK TO GUIDE)

BY

Dr P MAHADEVAN, RETIRED P.G Asst &

FORMER ASSISTANT PROFESSOR OF ENGLISH,

CHIDAMBARAM. 608001.

Let's chat

Made with ♥ on the Notion Press Platform

www.notionpress.com

About the Author

Dr.P.Mahadevan Parthasarathy Guptha is a former Assisant Professor of English, hailing from TAMILNADU State,Cuddalore District, Chidambaram town. He is passionate in learning and teaching.He had served in several capacities as Supervisor in School Education Department, PG.Asst of English in Govt.Hr.Sec.Schools, Vice Principal of a CBSE School, Principal of reputed Mat.Hr.Sec.Schools and finally as Assistant Professor of English in a Private B.Ed college in PONDICHERRY. Now he is acting as a trainer of Soft Skills and Life skills.

He has published a book already with the title,Varied Verses Viable Poems with an impressive message available in Amazon and Flipcart. Currently he is going to publish another book entitled, LET'S CHAT-SIMPLE STEPS TO SPEAK IN SPLENDID ENGLISH " with an intention to enable the rural youngsters to develop confidence and speak in English.This book is to be distributed FREE to the passionate beginners and differently abled students who wish to talk in English through their English teachers working in rural schools. He feels it's a part of his service to the student community.

He always sees the bright side of life. He is confident, strong and brave to face challenges in life. He radiates confidence, love and kindness in all his interactions with others.

He hopes that this present book will enable the aspiring students to talk in English confidently, improving their LSRW skills and essential vocabularies of the English language.

DEDICATION

To the interested beginners who want to speak in English.

FOREWORD

K.SETHUSUBRAMANIAN
Former Joint Director of Agriculture,
Secretary, Sri Gurugnana Sambandar Mission
Matric.Hr.Sec.School.
CHIDAMBARAM-608001

அன்பே சிவம்

I am happy to render a foreword to the book, "Let's chat" (Simaiesters.to Speak in splendid English) written by Dr.P.Mahadevan, former Principal of Sri Gurugnana Sambandar Mission Matric. Hr. Sec. School, Chidambaram and Assistant Professor of Krishnasamy College of Education (Women), Manappattu- Puducherry. He is well known to me for the past ten years and more.

He is an eminent teacher, educator and a prolific writer who strives for excellence. In this book he has left no stone unturned to make the beginners aspire to talk in English.

He has given easy, applicable tips to improve the core skills of English language in addition to some essential vocabularies to the passionate learners who wish to speak in English by practicing the different dialogues into conversational practice.

I do believe the impressive contents of the above book will benefit a lot to the readers who consistently follow the instructions given under each heading. I am confident that this book will receive good response from the students and other beginners who wish to speak in fluent English.

I wish the author all success in all his endeavours.

(K.SETHUSUBRAMANIAN)

FOREWORD

Mrs.V.SUGANDHI

Associate Professor

PG & Research Department of English

Thiruvalluvar Government Arts College

Rasipuram

In today's world, while physical distance no longer poses a barrier to people living at opposite ends of the globe, language still remains a significant challenge to effective communication. Although technologies like Google Translate and AI-powered tools have made it possible for people speaking different languages to connect, these translations often lack the warmth and personal touch of genuine conversation. Machine translations can sometimes be inaccurate or irrelevant, failing to capture the nuances of human interaction. Therefore, it is crucial for people to communicate in a common language. As we know, English has become the global lingua franca for communication.

Over the years, countless books have been written to help individuals improve their English communication skills. However, the book by Dr. P. Mahadevan stands out due to its unique approach. The idea and concept of this book have sprouted out of the difficulties he has seen people experience in their day to day and professional lives. As an English teacher, he felt compelled to share his knowledge and insights on teaching grammar, aiming to address common struggles faced by learners.

This book is organized into ten chapters, each thoughtfully structured by Dr. P. Mahadevan to guide readers from simpler to more complex concepts. This gradual progression makes understanding English grammar more accessible and less intimidating. The author goes beyond the traditional LSRW framework by incorporating Thinking Skills. The connection between Thinking Skills and LSRW is explored emphasizing how critical thinking plays a vital role in improving overall communication abilities. To enhance understanding, practical exercises are included, allowing readers to assess their own grasp of grammar and identify areas for improvement in their communication skills. The author includes a section on Common Phrasal Verbs, adding depth and variety to readers' vocabulary.

These phrasal verbs are categorized according to their usage, making it easier for readers to remember and apply them in the appropriate context.

Synonyms and antonyms, commonly used abbreviations with their full forms, vocabulary that is relevant to everyday communication, multiple meanings and synonyms for a single word thus enriching the readers' vocabulary and enhancing their ability to express themselves with precision, examples of all the major sentence structures and exercises designed to help learners master these patterns with confidence, outlining the key elements necessary for communication to be impactful and effective, practical tips along with useful phrases are some of the key elements provided to help readers strengthen their communication abilities. Dr. P. Mahadevan creates real-life scenarios and offers sample dialogues that might arise in these contexts. The "Tongue Twisters" chapter adds an element of fun while challenging readers to improve their pronunciation and fluency, making it both engaging and beneficial for those looking to refine their speaking skills.

This book stands out from others in its genre because it is written in clear, simple English, making it easy for readers to understand and follow the content. It avoids overwhelming or taxing the readers' concentration, offering a more accessible approach to learning. Practical exercises are included, allowing learners to actively practice and gain command over the language.

This book primarily focuses on helping rural students, who have limited exposure to English, develop the ability to communicate in a language understood globally. The use of simple language, clear expression of ideas, gradual progression of grammar concepts, and practical exercises serve the author's purpose. Together, these elements make the book a valuable resource for learners and a significant contribution to language education.

In addition to his roles as a school teacher and college professor, Dr. P. Mahadevan is also a poet and a writer known for his thought-provoking epigrammatic, concise, impactful sentences. He is highly respected and sought after by teachers, students, and scholars alike. Through his philanthropic efforts, Dr. Mahadevan continues to serve and enrich the teaching and learning community.

Associate Professor
PG & Research Department of English
Thiruvalluvar Government Arts College
Rasipuram

Acknowledgement

I am at first grateful to my parents Mr.V.Parthasarathy Guptha and Mrs.P.Pankajam who dedicated their lives to educate me and guide me.

I have much gratitude to my Spiritual Guru and inspirer Mr.K.Sethu Subramanian sir, Secretary, Sri Gurugnana Sambandhar M.M.Hr.Sec.School,Chidambaram for his kind fore ward to this book.

Next I wish to record my wholehearted thanks here to Mrs.P.R.Kalyani,B.T.Assistant for her invaluable selfless services in getting my books get published.

I am bound to thank extremely Mr.K.Manivasagam,Former Headmaster and Tamil Nadu State President of TNHSS PG Teachers Association who sowed the seed of writing this book within me at the time of my retirement from Govt.Service as P.G.Asst of English in GHSS,Kanur,Cuddalore district.

I thank whole heartedly all those teaching professionals and my wellwishers who have given their fore wards and reviews about this book.

 I thank profusely all my family members and close friends who have had an enormous impact on who I am now.

I am much obliged to the Notion Press Authorities for getting this beautiful book published in time.

CONTENTS   page no

Introduction

"Speaking in English is a powerful tool for personal and professional growth. "

I do hope the simple steps suggested in this booklet will help the beginners to acquire the basic skills of the English Language and start speaking in English.

I request them to put in consistent efforts to go through this booklet and practise the activities suggested in it. To master the art of speaking in English, one needs to develop their LSRW, (Listening, Speaking, Reading and Writing) skills of the English Language. Some simple tips and samples of dialogues are given in this booklet for this purpose and practice.

On perusing these materials, one can enhance their confidence and capabilities and career prospects. She/He can communicate well with different communities. There is no magic pill to master the art of speaking in English. Can we learn swimming without jumping into the water? Learn and understand the tips under LSRW skills and the Essential vocabularies and Verbs, Phrasal verbs and Sentence Patterns in English given in this booklet first. Then practise the dialogues given at the end of this booklet with your peers and friends consistently.

I do believe this booklet will inspire more students and enhance the rate of their personal success.

Come on, dear students,

"Dive into the pond of speaking in English and come out triumphantly. "

THE BEST WISHES, MAY GOD BLESS YOU!

Dr.P.Mahadevan

2. Basic Language skills

LISTENING SKILL

Listening is an art and if you are master in it, surely you are going to be a great speaker. A good Listener is always a good speaker. So, to improve listening skill listen to English news, English talks, English video clips at least ten minutes in the morning and ten minutes in the evening.

TIPS TO IMPROVE SPEAKING SKILL

"Our Attitude Determines Our Altitude"

Believe in yourself. Be self-confident that you can speak English well. Practice will make you Perfect.

Tips

• Speak in English with your teachers or friends for minimum 15minutes to 30 minutes daily.

• Observe the English speakers and repeat what they say to improve pronunciation and intonation.

• You need not be perfect in your speech in the beginning.

• Focus on your smooth communication only. Grammatical accuracy can be checked later on.

• Learn 5 to 10 new words or phrases daily to enhance your vocabulary.

• Use the newly learnt words or phrases in your daily life situations often, the repeated use of the vocabulary will help you remember them for a long time.

• Record your speech and listen to it and track progress.

• Participate in group discussions and learn from others.

• Usage of some idioms and phrasal verbs will help you speak more naturally.

• Read more books, journals and magazines to improve your vocabulary.

• Watch English movies and TV shows with sub titles at the bottom.

• Make note of what you watch and practise them in your speech.

• Practise saying Tongue Twisters several times.

• Don't be scared to make mistakes.

• Welcome mistakes, they are like old clothes that can be mended anytime.

• Try to describe the pictures in simple words.

• Speak about the weather in a few sentences.

• Introduce yourself in short.

• Narrate your everyday life briefly.

 You can't swim without jumping into the water.

Dive into the pond of speaking English and start speaking in English.

READING

Reading is also an art. If we read a lot, we will improve faster. Even if you read ten pages you can learn something new. It is better to read two pages and read carefully and try to understand them. You don't need to remember.

Why is Reading an important skill?

• It improves our vocabulary and knowledge.

• Increases our imagination and creativity.

• Lowers our stress and anxiety.

• Helps to relax and feel free.

• Our concentration and memory power increase.

• We learn more about life and locations.

• By reading more, our speaking skill will also get refined...

• Tips to improve Reading Skill

• Know your reading level and choose the correct materials.

• Set specific goals for your reading.

• Skim the text you want to read and see if it is interesting.

• Get a useful dictionary with synonyms and antonyms.

• Start reading simple articles in Newspapers in

English and proceed with reading English books.

Read a bunch of different materials, poems, prose and dramas.

• Read extensively and intensely.

• Start with loud reading first and move on to silent reading.

• Read the texts as quickly as possible.

• Try to learn five to ten new words or phrases daily while reading.

• Use them daily, in your real-life situations to remember them well.

• Make notes after reading a particular topic in the book or the article you read.

• Then reflect on the points you made after reading and check if any points are omitted with reference to the passages you read.

• Try to summarise what you read.

• Use bullet points to write the main ideas to understand the texts easily.

Identify the main ideas and supporting details.

• You may make use of the ICT, Information and Communication Technology for your reading too.

• Join a Reading Club if possible.

• Gradually expose yourself to different genres and authors.

• Mind mapping of the topic and content will be of great help to remember the points. (Example- A tree diagram depicting all points)

• Practise consistent reading habit and review and reflect on your progress

Reading Maketh a Ready man.

WRITING

In reading-part you read two pages.You have to take 8 to 12 correct grammatical sentences from these two pages and you have to write down in your notebook. Read them frequently. Try to remember the whole sentence rather than individual word meaning because if you know the complete sentence you can speak clearly and easily.

We need writing skill as it,

- helps to express our thoughts and feelings clearly.

- enables clear thinking.

- aids to recall memories.

- reduces stress.

- makes our mind active.

- assists to find our own voice and

- mostly it is a productive skill.

Tips to improve Writing skill

- Think first what you want to write about.
- Arrange your ideas logically.
- Write in simple sentences in the beginning
- Read some books on what you want to write about.
- Be precise in your writing.
- Review spelling and grammatical errors.
- Check the sentence structures.
- Read loudly what you wrote, while correcting the proof.
- Get feedback from one competent person.
- Attend some writing workshops.
- Start writing diary/ journal daily.

- Write letters to your friends and relatives frequently.

- Use strong form of verbs mostly

- Examples-run, see, write, draw

- Write in Active Voice form generally

- Vary your Sentence Patterns, kinds and sentence length gradually.

- Re read your writing and cut unnecessary words.

- Don't use cliches. (Repeatedly used words for long time)

- Enrich your vocabulary and use the new words you understood.

- Write one or two miracles you come across in your daily life in your diary.

- Start writing a Gratitude Journal thanking three different persons daily for their kind words and actions in your diary.

- Ensure your hand writing is neat and legible.

THINKING

Thinking is very important part of spoken English because whatever you can think, you can speak, so make a habit to think in English. Everything takes time, In the beginning it will be difficult but when you practice it will be a part of your memory and once it becomes your habit then English will come naturally from your mouth.

Mastering Minimum Vocabularies in English.

Minimum essential vocabularies under each part of speech are given below for your easy recalling, understanding and remembrance. You need not translate these words. For the vocabularies you don't understand the meaning kindly refer to a dictionary or search in google or you may ask your English teacher. Know the tense forms of the verbs.

3.Grammar with minimum Essential Vocabularies.

PARTS OF SPEECH

NOUN

A noun names a person, place, thing or idea.

EXAMPLE

Person-Maria, Boy, doctor

Place - Chennai, Park, Outer space.

Thing- pen, water melon, pencil

Idea- fairness, friendliness, acceptance

1.People

- Teacher
- Student
- Family
- Friend
- Doctor
- Engineer
- Artist
- Athlete
- Leader
- Community

2.Places

- School
- Home
- City
- Country

- Park
- Library
- Hospital
- Office
- Resturant
- Beach

3.Things

- Book
- Computer Phone
- Car
- Bike
- Music
- Art
- Food
- Sport
- Game

4.Food

- Fruit
- Vegetable
- Meat
- Bread
- Rice
- Pizza Sushi
- Coffee
- Tea
- Water

5.Emotions

- Joy
- Sadness
- Anger
- Fear

- Surprise
- Excitement
- Happiness
- Love
- Gratitude
- Sympathy

6.Miscellaneous

- Time
- money
- culture
- tradition
- history
- science
- technology
- environment
- economy
- government

7.animals

- Cat
- dog
- elephant
- fox
- goat
- horse
- jackal
- lion
- monkey
- ox

Exercise

1.After reading the nouns two or three times close the booklet and tell your friend some nouns you remember to your friend and ask him to tell some nouns. He/ She who tells the listener more nouns surely understood the nouns well. Read 20 words per day and test your understanding.

2.Find synonyms in English for any 10 words daily and write in a separate notebook. (Refer to a dictionary or search in Google or Ask your teacher)

PRONOUNS

Pronoun replaces the name of a person, place, thing or idea in a sentence.
Examples
1.You
2.We
3.They
4.He
5.She
6.Me
7.It
8.Him
9.Her
10..This
11.That
12.Those
13.These
14.Each

Personal Pronouns

1. I
2. me
3. you
4. he
5.him
6. she
7. her
8. it
9. we
10. us

11. they
12. them
13. my
14. mine
15. your
16. yours
17. his
18. hers
19. its

20. **our**

Demonstrative Pronouns

1. this

2. that

3. these

4. those

5. here

6. there

7. now

8. then

9. thus

10. hence

Interrogative Pronouns

1. who

2. what

3. which

4. whom

5. whose

6. whoever

7. whatever

8. whichever

9. whomever

10. whatever

Indefinite Pronouns

1. someone

2. something

3. anyone

4. anything

5. nobody

6. nothing

7. everyone

8. everything

9. all

10. both

11. each

12. few

13. many

14. several

15. some

16. any

17. nobody

18. everyone

19. either

20. neither.

These pronouns are commonly used in everyday conversation, writing, and reading.

Exercise

1.Read the pronouns twice or thrice and practice with your peers and friends.

2. Test yourselves who knows more pronouns.

3.Closing the booklet, write 10 pronouns without seeing the booklet.

ADJECTIVES

An adjective describes a noun or pronoun.

Example

Size/shape: tiny, long, oval

Texture: prickly, smooth, leathery

Odor/tasty: nutty, flowery, sour

Appearance: bright, beautiful, faded

Positive Adjectives

1. Good

2. Great

3. Excellent

4. Fantastic

5. Amazing

6. Beautiful

7. Happy

8. Friendly

9. Kind

10. Helpful

11. Honest

12. Intelligent

13. Creative

14. Innovative

15. Successful

16. Confident

17. Determined

18. Strong

19. Courageous

20. Resilient

21. Vibrant

22. Colourful

23. Joyful

24. Harmonious

25. Peaceful

26. Serene

27. Tranquil

28. Calm

29. Gentle

30. Sincere

31. Warm

32. Welcoming

33. Generous

34. Thoughtful

35. Considerate

36. Polite

37. Respectful

38. Admirable

39. Inspiring

40. Uplifting

41. Charming

42. Delightful

43. Elegant

44. Sophisticated

45. Refined

46. Loyal

47. Devoted

48. Faithful

49. Trustworthy

50.Reliable

Negative Adjectives

1. Bad

2. Terrible

3. Awful

4. Poor

5. Unhappy

6. Unfriendly

7. Harsh

8. Cruel

9. Dishonest

10. Unfair

11. Weak

12. Fragile

13. Delicate

14. Difficult

15. Challenging

16. Demanding

17. Stressful

18. Anxious

19. Worrisome

20. Frightening

Descriptive Adjectives

1. Big

2. Small

3. Tall

4. Short

5. Fat

6. Thin

7. Old

8. Young

9. New

10. Old

11. Fast

12. Slow

13. Hot

14. Cold

15. Bright

16. Dim

17. Light

18. Heavy

19. Soft

20. Hard

21. Smooth

22. Rough

23. Round

24. Square

25. Rectangular

Quantitative Adjectives

1. Many

2. Few

3. Several

4. Some

5. Any

6. All

7. Both

8. Each

9. Every

10. Enough

These adjectives are commonly used in everyday conversation, writing, and reading.

Exercise

1.   Read the Adjectives twice or thrice and understand them by referring to the synonyms or meanings with reference to dictionary or Google search or consulting your teacher.

2.   Write 10 different Adjectives in your notebook without seeing the booklet daily.

 3.Have a companion for discussion of the adjectives daily 20 at least. Whoever knows more adjectives is better in understanding the adjectives.

VERB

A verb tells a noun's action or state of being.

Example

Action

Ask, jump, think, want, run, dance, eat, fix

State of being

Is, are, be, have, was, were

Action Verbs

1. Run

2. Jump

3. Read

4. Write

5. Speak

6. Listen

7.Learn

8. Teach

9. Play

10. Work

11. Create

12. Imagine

13. Build

14. Design

15. Develop

16. Plan

17.Organize

18. Manage

19. Lead

20. Follow

21. Help

22. Support

23. Assist

24. Guide

25. Mentor

26. Share

27. Discuss

28. Debate

29. Decide

30. Act

31. React

32. Respond

33. Interact

34. Engage

35. Participate

36. Contribute

37.Collaborate

38.Cooperate

39.Compete

40.Achieve

41.Succeed

42. Fail

43. Improve

44. Enhance

45.. Refine

46.. Simplify

47. Clarify

48. Explain

49.. Demonstrate

50.Illustrate

Communication Verbs

1.Say

2.Tell

3Ask

4.Answer

5.Discuss

6.Debate

7.Converse

8.Chat

9. Talk

10. Listen

11. Hear

12. Understand

13. Agree

14. Disagree

15. Argue

16. Persuade

17. Convince

18. Encourage

19. Motivate

20. Inspire

21. Educate

22. Inform

23.Explain

24. Describe

25. Narrate

26. Report

27. Announce

28. Declare

29. Propose

30. Suggest

3. Emotional Verbs

1. Love

2. Hate

3. Like

4. Dislike

5. Enjoy

6. Suffer

7. Feel

8. Think

9. Believe

10. Doubt

11. Fear

12. Hope

13. Wish

14. Desire

15. Need

16. Want

17. Prefer

18. Choose

19. Regret

20. Forgive

4. Cognitive Verbs

1. Know

2. Understand

3. Learn

4. Remember

5. Forget

6. Recognize

7. Identify

8. Analyze

9. Evaluate

10. Assess

11. Compare

12. Contrast

13. Reason

14. Deduce

15. Infer

16. Conclude

17. Decide

18. Judge

19. Consider

20. Reflect

5. State Verbs

1. Be

2. Have

3. Exist

4. Appear

5. Seem

6. Remain

7. Stay

8. Continue

9. Last

10. Endure

11. Survive

12. Thrive

13. Grow

14. Develop

15. Improve

16. Deteriorate

17. Decline

18. Incease

19. Decrease

20. Change

6.Miscellaneous Verbs

1. Travel

2. Move

3. Live

4. Stay

5. Visit

6. Explore

7. Discover

8. Invent

9. Create

10. Innovate

11. Adapt

12. Overcome

13. Achieve

14. Succeed

15. Fail

16. Recover

17. Restore

18. Renew

19. Revise

20. Edit

21. Publish

22. Share

23. Present

24. Demonstrate

25. Explain

26. Illustrate

27. Describe

28. Narrate

29. Report

30. Announce

These verbs are commonly used in everyday conversation, writing, and reading.

Exercise.

1.Read all the Verbs twice or thrice.

2.They are the action words very useful in speaking and writing for communication.

3.Find out synonym at least one for each word and write in your note book. Minimum for 20 words a day.

They will enhance your vocabularies.

4.Find out the other two tense forms of the given verbs with the help of your teachers or Google search and note them down in your notebook.

5.Try to use and understand minimum ten verbs in your real life situations.

6. Test your understanding and knowledge of verbs with your friend or peer ready to learn with you.

ADVERBS

What are Adverbs?

Adverbs modify verbs, adjectives, or other adverbs to indicate manner, time, place, frequency, or degree.

Examples:

1.Quickly

2.Yesterday

3.Here

4.Often

5.Extremely

Time Adverbs

1. Now

2. Then

3. Soon

4. Later

5. Early

6. Late

7. Already

8. Yet

9. Recently

10. Previously

11. Currently

12. Immediately

13. Quickly

14. Slowly

15. Gradually

16. Suddenly

17. Unexpectedly

18. Frequently

19. Occasionally

20. Rarely

Manner Adverbs

1. Well

2. Badly

3. Fast

4. Slowly

5. Carefully

6. Wisely

7. Foolishly

8. Kindly

9. Gently

10. Harshly

11. Loudly

12. Softly

13. Clearly

14. Confusedly

15. Politely

16. Rudely

17. Patiently

18. Impatiently

19. Calmly

20. Angrily

Place Adverbs

1. Here

2. There

3. Everywhere 4. Nowhere

5. Somewhere

6. Anywhere

7. Up

8. Down

9. In

10. Out

11. On

12. Off

13. Over

14. Under

15. Above

16. Below

17. Beside

18. Between

19. Among

20. Throughout

Frequency Adverbs

1. Always

2. Never

3. Often

4. Seldom

5. Rarely

6. Usually

7. Normally

8. Occasionally

9. Sometimes

10. Frequently

11. Infrequently

12. Constantly

13. Continuously

14. Periodically

15. Regularly

16. Irregularly

17. Randomly

18. Intermittently

19. Sporadically

20. Consistently

Degree Adverbs

1. Very

2. Extremely

3. Highly

4. Quite

5. Rather

6. Somewhat

7. Slightly

8. Moderately

9. Considerably

10. Significantly

11. Substantially

12. Noticeably

13. Remarkably

14. Exceptionally

15. Extraordinarily

16. Unusually

17. Abnormally

18. Excessively

19. Insufficiently

20. Adequately

These adverbs are commonly used in everyday conversation, writing, and reading.

Exercise:

1.   Read 20 adverbs daily, find meaning and synonyms for them and write them in your notebook.

2.   Test your knowledge about Adverbs with your co learner daily about the 20 adverbs you learned.

3.Use them whenever possible in your daily real-life situations.

PREPOSITIONS

A preposition shows the relationship, such as direction, time, or placement between a noun or pronoun and another word in a sentence.

Example

1. About
2. Across
3. After
4. Around
5. Before
6. Between
7. Into
8. Through
9. to

Location Prepositions

1. In (The book is in the library.)

2. On (The picture is on the wall.)

3. At (Meet me at the station.)

4. By (The river flows by the city.)

5. With (She's standing with her friends.)

6. Under (The cat is under the bed.)

7. Above (The plane is flying above the clouds.)

8. Over (The bridge goes over the river.)

9. Across (The street runs across the town.)

10. Through (The train goes through the tunnel.)

11.Between (The park is between the two buildings.)

12. Among (The flowers are among the trees.)

13. Beside (The hotel is beside the beach.)

14. Along (The road runs along the coast.)

15. Around (The city is surrounded by mountains.)

16. Opposite (The restaurant is opposite the theatre)

17. Near (The hotel is near the airport.)

18. Far (The city is far from the countryside.)

19. Beyond (The mountains stretch beyond the horizon.)

20. Within (The park is within walking distance.)

Direction Prepositions

1. To (I'm going to the store.)

2. From (I'm coming from school.)

3. Up (The stairs go up to the second floor.)

4. Down (The elevator goes down to the basement.)

5. In (Enter the building through the front door.)

6. Out (Let's go out for dinner.)

7. Through (The road goes through the forest.)

8. Across (The ferry goes across the lake.)

9. Along (The bike path runs along the river.)

10. Back (I'm going back home.)

Time Prepositions

1. At (Meet me at 5 o'clock.)

2. On (My birthday is on July 12th.)

3. During (I'll be on vacation during August.)

4. Before (Let's meet before the movie.)

5. After (I'll see you after class.)

6. Until (I'll work until 5 o'clock.)

7. Since (I've been studying since morning.)

8. For (I'll be away for three days.)

9. During (The sale is during the holidays.)

10. By (Finish the project by Friday.)

Other Prepositions

1. About (The book is about history.)

2. Of (A cup of coffee.)

3. With (I'm going with my friends.)

4.From (I got a letter from my sister.)

5. Under (The company is under new management.)

6. Within (The answer is within the text.)

7. Without (I'm going without breakfast.)

8. Throughout (The festival is throughout the city.)

9. Despite (I'll go despite the rain.)

10.Regarding (I have questions regarding the project.)

PREPOSITIONAL PHRASES

1. In front of

2. Behind the

3. Next to

4. On top of

5. Underneath

6. Inside

7. Outside

8. Across from

9. Alongside

10. Throughout

These are some prepositions and prepositional phrases commonly used in everyday conversation, writing, and reading.

Exercise:

1.Read the above prepositions and prepositional phrases and understand their meanings used in the example sentences given within the brackets..

2.Try to use that preposition in another sentence changing the nouns in that sentence.

3.After reading all of them test your knowledge in Preposition with your co learner.

4.Use any 5 five prepositions in your own sentences and write in your note book.

CONJUNCTIONS

A conjunction joins two ideas or shows the relationship between two parts of a sentence.

Example

1. And
2. Because
3. But
4. So
5. Through
6. Or
7. Until
8. While
9. Unless

Coordinating Conjunctions

1. And (I like reading books, and I also enjoy watching movies.)

2. But (I wanted to go, but I was too tired.)

3. Or (Do you want coffee or tea?)

4. So (I'm tired, so I'm going to bed.)

5. Yet (I'm tired, yet I still need to finish this work.)

6. For (I'm going to the store, for I need milk.)

7. Nor (I don't like coffee, nor do I like tea.)

8. Either…or (Either you come with me, or you stay home.)

9. Not only…but also (I not only like reading, but also writing.)

10.Both…and (I like both coffee and tea.)

Subordinating Conjunctions

1. Because (I'm tired because I didn't sleep well.)

2. Since (I've been busy since morning.)

3. After (I'll go for a walk after I finish dinner.)

4. Before (Let's meet before the movie starts.)

5. Until (I'll work until I finish this project.)

6. Unless (I won't go unless you come with me.)

7. Although (I'm tired, although I slept well.)

8. Though (I'm tired, though I slept well.)

9. If (I'll go if you want me to.)

10. Provided (I'll go, provided you come with me.)

Correlative Conjunctions

1. Both…and (I like both coffee and tea.)

2. Either…or (Either you come with me, or you stay home.)

3. Not only…but also (I not only like reading, but also writing.)

4. Whether…or (Whether you like it or not, we're going.)

5. As…as (He's as tall as his brother.)

Concessive Conjunctions

1. Although (I'm tired, although I slept well.)

2. Though (I'm tired, though I slept well.)

3. Even though (I'm tired, even though I slept well.)

4. Despite (I'll go, despite the rain.)

5. However (I'm tired; however, I still need to finish this work.)

Conjunctional Phrases

1. As long as

2. As soon as

3. As well as

4. In order that

5. Provided that

6. So that

7. Unless otherwise

8. Until then

9. Whereas

10. While

These conjunctions are commonly used in everyday conversation, writing, and reading.

Exercises:

1.Read all the above conjunctions and conjunctional phrases and understand the meanings of them by reading the example sentences and consulting your English teachers.

2.   Try to frame similar sentences of the example sentences for any 5 conjunctions daily and write them down in your notebook.

3.   Test your knowledge about conjunctions with your co learner daily.

INTERJECTIONS

An interjection expresses a strong emotion and is often followed by an exclamation point.

Examples

1. Ah
2. Hurry up!
3. Well
4. Hey Bravo
5. Oh no!

Emotional Interjections

1. Oh! (Oh! I forgot my phone.)

2. Wow! (Wow! That's amazing!)

3. Ah! (Ah! I understand now.)

4. Ouch! (Ouch! That hurts!)

5. Yay! (Yay! I'm so excited!)

6. Boo! (Boo! You scared me!)

7. Ugh! (Ugh! This food is disgusting!)

8. Hmm (Hmm, I'm not sure.)

9. Ahh (Ahh, that feels good.)

10. Oops (Oops, I made a mistake.)

11. Whoa! (Whoa! That's crazy!)

12. Whoo… (Whoo... Let's go!)

13. Yeah! (Yeah! I agree!)

14. No! (No! Don't do that!)

15. Okay! (Okay! I'll do it.)

16. Wowzer! (Wowzer! That's incredible!)

17. Geez! (Geez! That's amazing!)

18. Jeez! (Jeez! That's crazy!)

19. Gosh! (Gosh! I'm surprised!)

20. Goodness! (Goodness! That's wonderful!)

Greeting Interjections

1. Hello! (Hello! How are you?)

2. Hi! (Hi! What's up?)

3. Hey! (Hey! Long time no see!)

4. Hiya! (Hiya! How's it going?)

5. Heya! (Heya! What's new?)

6. Welcome! (Welcome! Come on in!)

7. Congratulations! (Congratulations! You did it!)

8. Happy birthday! (Happy birthday! Have a great day!)

9. Merry Christmas! (Merry Christmas! Happy holidays!)

10. Happy New Year! (Happy New Year! Cheers to a new year!)

Exclamatory Interjections

1. Fantastic! (Fantastic! I'm so happy!)

2. Amazing! (Amazing! That's incredible!)

3. Incredible! (Incredible! That's awesome!)

4. Unbelievable! (Unbelievable! That's crazy!)

5. Awesome! (Awesome! That's amazing!)

6. Brilliant! (Brilliant! That's genius!)

7. Excellent! (Excellent! Well done!)

8. Exceptional! (Exceptional! You're the best!)

9. Outstanding! (Outstanding! That's impressive!)

10.Superb! (Superb! That's fantastic!)

Other Interjections

1. Shh! (Shh! Be quiet.)

2. Psst! (Psst! Come here.)

3. Oops! (Oops! My mistake.)

4. Ahem! (Ahem! Excuse me.)

5. Uh-oh! (Uh-oh! Something's wrong.)

6. Oh no! (Oh no! That's terrible!)

7. Oh dear! (Oh dear! That's unfortunate!)

8. Good grief! (Good grief! That's shocking!)

9. Goodness gracious! (Goodness gracious! That's amazing!)

10. For Pete's sake! (For Pete's sake! Come on!)

These interjections are commonly used in everyday conversation, writing, and reading.

Exercise:

1.Read the above interjections twice or thrice and understand when to use them with reference to the example sentences given in brackets after them.

2.Use any five interjections in your real life daily situations and write them in your note book.

3. Test your knowledge about Interjections with your co learner any 10 interjections daily.

COMMON PHRASAL VERBS

Movement Phrasal Verbs

1. Get on (Get on the bus at the next stop.)

2. Get off (Get off the train at the last stop.)

3. Go up (The elevator will go up to the top floor.)

4. Come down (Come down from the ladder carefully.)

5. Turn left/right (Turn left at the next intersection.)

6. Move in (They're moving in next door tomorrow.)

7. Move out (I'm moving out of the apartment next month.)

8. Walk in/out (Walk in and take a seat.)

9. Run into (I ran into an old friend at the party.)

10. Drive by (Drive by the park on your way home.)

Action Phrasal Verbs

11. Pick up (Pick up the phone and answer it.)

12. Put down (Put down the book and rest.)

13. Take off (Take off your shoes before entering.)

14. Give up (I give up; it's too hard.)

15. Get together (Let's get together for dinner tonight.)

16. Break down (The car broke down on the highway.)

17. Build up (The company is building up its reputation.)

18. Clean up (Clean up the mess before you leave.)

19. Fill out (Fill out the application form.)

20. Hand in (Hand in your homework by tomorrow.)

Communication Phrasal Verbs

1. Call back (Call back later; I'm busy.)

2. Write down (Write down the address and phone number.)

3. Read up (Read up on the latest news.)

4. Talk over (Let's talk over the plans.)

5. Listen in (Listen in on the conversation.)

6. Speak up (Speak up; I can't hear you.)

7. Answer back (Answer back when your name is called.)

8. Join in (Join in the conversation.)

9. Keep in touch (Keep in touch with old friends.)

10. Look up (Look up the word in the dictionary.)

Time and Schedule Phrasal Verbs

1. Get ahead (Get ahead of schedule.)

2. Fall behind (I'm falling behind on my work.)

3. Catch up (Catch up on your sleep.)

4. Slow down (Slow down; you're driving too fast.)

5.   Speed up (Speed up; we are running late.)

6.   Put off (Put off the meeting until tomorrow.)

7.   Postpone (Postpone the party until next week.)

8.   Bring forward (Bring forward the meeting to today.)

9.   Take time off (Take time off from work.)

10.   Turn in (Turn in your project by the deadline.)

Other Phrasal Verbs

1.   Give away (Give away your old clothes.)

2.   Throw away (Throw away the trash.)

3.   Look forward (I look forward to seeing you.)

4.   Care for (Do you care for coffee or tea?)

5.   Go through (Go through the tunnel.)

6.   Hold on (Hold on to your seat.)

7.   Keep on (Keep on working.)

8.   Make up (Make up your mind.)

9.   Point out (Point out the mistake.)

10.   Stand out (Stand out from the crowd.)

These phrasal verbs are commonly used in everyday conversation, writing, and reading.

Exercise:

1.   Read all the above phrasal verbs twice or thrice and understand their meanings with reference to the example sentences given within brackets after each of them.

2.   Try to use any 5 phrasal verbs in your daily life situations and write them down in your note book.

3.   Test your knowledge in phrasal verbs with your co learner five phrasal verbs daily.

Speaking phrases

1.Saying, 'I think'.

- If you ask me
- I honestly believe that
- It's my belief that
- To my way of thinking
- My point of view is
- As far as I can tell
-

2.Saying 'Because'

- Considering
- Due to
- For the reason that
- For the sake
- In as much as
- In behalf of
- In that
- In the interest of
-

3.Saying 'You are welcome'

- Certainly
- Cool It's all gravy
- My pleasure
- Not at all
- Glad to be of any assistance
- Don't mention it
- You got it

Saying 'Well done'

- way to go
- marvellous
- good for you
- well,
- look at you
- go tremendous
- I am impressed
- You did it that time
- You are really improving

Saying 'No'

- No thanks, I have another
- I'd love to…but can't I wish, I could make it work
- May be another time
- I am sorry, I am busy
- I am already booked
- That's not going to work for me

Saying 'Thankyou'

- That's so kind of you
- Many thanks
- I can't thank you enough
- All my love and thanks to you

- Words can't describe how thankful I am
- Thanks a ton for helping out
- cheers

Saying 'Hello!'

- Hey how are you feeling today?
- bonjour
- howdy
- how are ya?
- Long time no see
- Good to see you
- Greetings
- Hey there

4.SYNONYMS.

1. Happy- joyful
2. Sad-unhappy
3. Fast-quick
4. Slow-sluggish
5. Bright-luminous
6. Dark-gloomy
7. Strong-powerful
8. Weak-feeble
9. Large-big
10. Small-tiny
11. Hot-warm
12. cold-chilly
13. rich-wealthy
14. poor-impoverished
15. easy-simple
16. difficult-hard
17. clean-pristine
18. dirty-filthy
19. healthy-fit
20. calm-peaceful
21. angry-furious
22. bright-vivid
23. dull-boring
24. expensive-costly
25. cheap-inexpensive
26. generous-kind
27. friendly-amiable
28. hostile-unfriendly

29. honest-truthful
30. curious- inquisitive
31. lucky-fortunate
32. tired-exhausted
33. energetic-lively
34. hungry-starving
35. thirsty-parched
36. polite-courteous
37. rude-impolite
38. common-ordinary

5.ANTONYMS

1. Enjoy X hate
2. Enter X leave Entrance(exit)
3. Equal X different
4. Even X odd
5. Excited X calm
6. Exciting X boring
7. Exclude X include
8. Exit X entrance
9. Final X first
10. Find X lose
11. Finish X begin
12. Finish X start
13. First X final
14. Fix X break
15. Flat X hilly
16. Floor X ceiling
17. Follow X lead
18. Forbid X allow
19. Form X destroy
20. Fortune X mis fortune
21. Fresh X old/stale
22. Harvest X plant

23. Healthy X ill Health(disease)

24. Heaven X hell

25. Heavy X light

26. Hell X heaven

27. Host X guest

28. Huge X tiny
29. Human X animal

30. Humane X cruel

31. Humid X dry

32. Hungry X full

33. Husband X wife
34. Front X back
35. Ignore X notice

36. Import X export

37. In X out

38. Include X exclude

39. Life X death

40. Light X dark

41. Like X hate

42. Little X big

43. Little X much

44. Live X die

45. Long X short
46. Lose X win

6. Abbreviations

1.	Mr	Mister
2.	Mrs	Mistress
3.	Ms	Miss
4.	Jr	Junior
5.	Sr	Senior
6.	Dr	Doctor
7.	Rd	Road
8.	St	Street
9.	Corp	Corporation
10.	In	Inch
11.	Cm	Centimeter
12.	Blvd	Boulvard
13.	AD	Anno Domini
14.	BC	Before Christ

7.Descriptive words

1. Absorbing
2. Admirable
3. Affluent
4. Amiable
5. Amazing
6. Amusing
7. Amused
8. Amusing
9. Astonishing
10. Awful
11. Awesome
12. Breathe taking
13. Brilliant
14. Blissful
15. Bright
16. Bad
17. Captivating
18. Charming
19. Cheerful
20. Comical
21. Contented
22. Congenial
23. Considerate
24. Courteous
25. Compelling
26. Crummy
27. Deep
28. Decisive
29. Delightful
30. Despicable
31. Disagreeable
32. Disgraceful
33. Dreadful

34. Diverting
35. Eager
36. Engaging
37. Engrossing
38. Enjoyable
39. Entertaining
40. Enthralling
41. Entertaining
42. Enthusiastic
43. Eventful
44. Extensive
45. Essential
46. Extraordinary
47. Fabulous
48. Fantastic
49. Farcical
50. Fat
51. Fundamental
52. Funny
53. Great
54. Gleeful
55. Goofy
56. Gracious
57. Great
58. Gloomy
59. Good
60. Happy
61. Hateful
62. Heart broken
63. Heavy
64. Hilarious
65. Humorous
66. Historical
67. Horrible
68. Incredible
69. Interesting

70. Important
71. Imperative
72. Lousy
73. Little
74. Loaded
75. Major
76. Marvelous
77. Melancholy
78. Mini
79. Miniature
80. Minute
81. Miserable
82. Mournful
83. Naughty
84. Nice
85. Outstanding
86. Opulent
87. Petite
88. Prosperous
89. Pleasant
90. Rich
91. Sombre
92. Sorrowful
93. Splendid
94. Stupendous
95. Small
96. Skimpy
97. Slight
98. Teeny-weeny
99. Tiny

100. Wealthy

8.SENTENCE PATTERN

Here are some basic sentence patterns in English, along with examples:

1. Subject-Verb-Object (SVO)

Example: "She eats breakfast."

2. Subject-Verb-Adjunct (SVA)

Example: "He drives carefully."

3. Subject-Verb-Complement (SVC)

Example: "The water is cold."

4. Subject-Verb-Indirect Object-Direct Object (SVIODO)

Example: "She gave him a gift."

5.Subject, Verb, Direct Object. Indirect Object, Adjunct (SVDOIOA)

Example " My father gave me a watch yesterday.

6.Subject-Verb-Object-Prepositional Phrase (SVO-PP)

Example: "She put the book on the table."

7.Subject-Verb-Adverb-Prepositional Phrase (SVA-PP)

Example: "He walked slowly across the room."

8.Subject-Verb-Object-Adjunct (SVOA)

Example: "She sings songs beautifully."

9.Subject, Verb, Complement, Adjunct. (SVCA)

Example: My niece is a doctor now.

These sentence patterns are the building blocks of English grammar, and mastering them will help you construct clear and correct sentences in English.

Exercise:

1.Read the above basic Sentence Patterns with examples twice or thrice and understand them well.

2. Write 2 simple sentences like the example sentences for 2 Sentence Patterns in your note book daily.

3.Test your knowledge in Sentence Patterns with your co learner.

9.EFFECTIVE COMMUNICATION SKILLS

There are two types of communication

1. Verbal Communication: Speaking clearly, using appropriate tone, pitch, and volume.

2. Nonverbal Communication: Facial expressions, body language, eye contact, and gestures.

a. Maintain Effective Eye Contact

b. Use your voice well.

c. Make your body language persuasive

d. Grab the Audiences' Attention.

Communication skills comprise of all the above four skills. With the knowledge of the above four skills and minimum vocabularies we can start speaking in English and communicate effectively by managing our,

* Physical behaviour

* Vocal behaviour and

* Verbal behaviour.

Conversation is the principal tool for Communication. Simple Seven ways to improve your communication skills.

State your objectives clearly at the start.

Think twice before you speak.

Manage the Time correctly.

Find a common good for both speakers.

Stay away from arguments.

Summarise your points now and then.

Use Visuals like mind maps and metaphors etc.

Developing strong communication skills can enhance personal and professional growth, Interpersonal relationships and promote successful interactions in various contexts.

Minimum vocabularies, some Phrasal verbs, Sentence

Patterns, some Dialogues for conversational practice as Role plays in different contexts and Tongue Twisters etc, are given in the

following pages for some exercises and activities are given at the bottom of each sub topics. If you consistently practise these ideas, You will definitely become a better speaker in English.

IMPORTANT INSTRUCTIONS.

Let us come to the most important part of this booklet that enables you to start speaking in English.

1.Drive away your shyness and start speaking in English.

2. Spare at least 30 minutes to 1hr daily for speaking practice in English with one co learner who is also interested to speak in English.

3.Find that passionate co learner or well-wisher who can respond to you in English.

4.Practise all the small dialogues given in this booklet with your co learner, one dialogue a day.

5.Dialogue is the written form of the conversation.

6. When you practise the dialogue as conversational practice, your speaking skill in English develops naturally.

7. You may practise these dialogues by seeing them for the first and second time and the third time without seeing.

8.Practise each dialogue 5 times or as many times until you both are confident to speak that dialogue without mistakes, seeing the dialogue.

9. Try to read the dialogues and understand them well and start to speak in English with your co learner.

10. Dialogues in different contexts are given in this booklet for your practice.

11. Consistently practise them, daily one dialogue at least or as many as you can for 2 months without break. You will surely become a speaker in English soon.

DIALOGUES FOR COVERSATIONAL PRACTICE

Replace the letter A with the speaker's name, and B with the co speaker's name in the dialogues where ever necessary and address them and address them by his /her name as he/she is your peer. If elder address as brother or sister or sir/madam accordingly.

1.Formal greetings in the morning school 1.Greeting the headmaster/teacher

A: Happy morning. How are you sir/mam

B: Happy morning A, how about you?

A: I am fine, Thank you sir /mam

B: Had your breakfast?

A: Yes, sir/ mam

B: shall we start the class

A: Yes, sir/ mam

2.Greeting friends (peers. Equals, friends)

A: Hello, happy morning B, how are you?

B: Hello happy morning A, how about you?

A: Fine, Thank you, how about you?

B; fine, thank you, had your breakfast?

A: Yes, It's time, shall we go to the class.

B: yes, by all means…

3.Introducing

(A with your name, and B with your co learner's name)

A: Hello B, Happy morning…, meet my father.

B: Hello, happy morning (Name). What's your father?

A: He is a____ (farmer, carpenter, tailor)

B: Glad

 A: Where are you going?

A: We are on the way to -------(bank, post office, market, etc) B

B: Ok, take care A.

4. Ordering coffee

(A with your name, and B with your co learner's name)

A: Shall I have a coffee, please?

B: Would you like sugar or cream?

A: Half sugar please.

B: Would you like strong coffee or light coffee?

A: I prefer medium coffee please.

B: Please wait, it will come soon.

A: Sure, Thank you.

5.Shoppping

A:(coming into the shop)

B: Welcome sir, what do you want?

A: I wish to buy a cotton shirt? How much it cost?

B: It costs Rs. 750 sir.

A: Shall I have a blue colour shirt?

B: Ok, by all means, Here it is sir.

A: nice, pack this shirt please.

B: sure sir, kindly go to the counter and pay your bill sir,

Then collect your shirt from the delivery cabin.

A: sure, thank you.

6.Making a reservation in a hotel

A; Do you have a table for two at 8pm today?

B: Yes, we do, What's your name?

A: I am A.

B: Your phone number please…

 A: Its 34556121.

B: Table number 5 reserved sir.

7.Talking about weather

A: Nice weather today, Is'nt it?

B: Yes Its beautiful.

A: Is it chill or warm?

B: Neither chill, nor warm.

A: Its pleasant, let us enjoy it.

B: That's good

8. Asking for help

A: Can you help me please?

B: Of course, What do you need?

A: I want to go to the railway station.

B: Better, hire an auto its far away.

A: Okay, Thank you.

9.Asking for direction

A: Excuse me, where is the rest room?

B: Its down the hall, second door on your left.

A: Is there lift facilities here?

B: Sorry, no lifts available here.

A: ok, thank you.

10. Saying, 'Goodbye'.

A: See you later, I have some work.

B: When shall we meet again?

A: Tomorrow, Are you free?

B: Yes, I will be free.

A: Fine, Lets meet tomorrow.

B: Good bye, Have a great day.

11.Making a complaint

A: This food is good.

B: I apologize, let me get you a new plate.

A: Can I order a new item please.

B: By all means, sir /mam.

A: Thank you.

12.Asking for advice

A: What do you think I should do?

B: I think, you should try…

A: What shall ai do now?

B: Refer a standard dictionary.

A: Ok sir, I will, thank you.

13.Talking about a movie

A: have you seen that movie?

B: Yes, It's great.

A: Are the comedies enjoyable?

B: Yes Of course.

A: yeah, I like comedies, sure, I will watch this movie.

14. Asking Permission

 A: Can I use your phone?

B: Yes, Take this.

A: Only 5 minutes I need.

B: Yes, but in my presence.

A: Sure, Thank you so much.

15.Talking about a hobby.

A: Do you like reading?

B: Yes, I love it.

A: Do you love novels?

B: Yes, Novels, Who is your favourite?

A; I like Charles Dickens,

B: Good, I too.

16. Asking for the time

A: What time is it?

B: Its 3pm.

A; Thankyou, how long will it take to reach the railway station?

B: It may take an hour.

A: Ok, Thank you.

17. Making a suggestion

A: "Let's go to the park."

B: "That sounds like fun."

A: Why do you say so?

B: It's already 8 pm.

A: Shall we go tomorrow evening?

B. Sure. We shall...

18. Talking about a trip

A: "Where did you go on vacation?"

B: "I went to the beach."

A: To which beach?

B: To Marina beach in Chennai.

A: Glad to hear. How is it?

B: It's very beautiful.

19.Asking for a recommendation

A: Do you know a good restaurant?

B: Yes, try Hotel Annamalai.

A:ls that a Vegetarian one?

B: yes, yes.

A: Thank you.

20.Talking about a book

A: "Have you read that book?"

B: "Yes, it's amazing."

A: What is the theme?

B: The themes are loyalty and friendship.

A: How is the language style?

B: Simple and clear!

21.Making an apology

A: "I'm so sorry I'm late."

B: "It's okay, don't worry about it.

A: What happened?

B: I met with a minor accident.

A: Got injured?

B: No, Thanks to God.

22.At the Airport

A: (Traveler): Excuse me, where is the check-in counter for Flight BA 123?

B (Airport Staff): It's just down that hall, on your left.

A: Thank you. And where do I go after checking in?

B: Proceed to security checkpoint C.

A: Okay, got it.

B: Have a safe flight!

A: Thank you, sir.

23.In a Coffee Shop

A:(Customer): Hi, I'd like a large coffee with cream.

B:(Server): Would you like whole milk or skim milk?

A: Whole milk, please.

B: That'll be Rs.35/-

A: Here you go.

B: Thank you, enjoy!

24.At the Bank

A(Customer): Hi, I'd like to open a new savings account.

B(Banker): Great! Give me some information please

A: Okay.

B: What's your ID and proof of address?

A: Here you go.

B: Alright, I'll open a Savings Bank Account for you.

B: Thankyou sir.

25. In a Store

A(Customer): Do you have this shirt in a larger size?

B(Salesman): Let me check. (pause)

Yes, we have it in XL.

A: Great, where is it?

B: Aisle 3.

A: Thanks!

B: Need any help to find it out?

A: No, I'll manage sir.

26. On the Phone

A(Caller): Hi, I'm calling about the apartment for rent.

B(Landlord): Ah, yes! It's still available.

A: Great. Can I have a viewing?

B: How about tomorrow at 2 PM?

A: That works out well.

B: See you then.

27. Social Gathering (Introductions)

A (Host): Hey, I'm.........(name).

B (Guest): Nice to meet you, I'm ______(Name)

A: Welcome to our home.

B: Thanks, it's lovely.

A: Can I get you a drink?

B: Just water, please.

28.Doctor's clinic

A:(Doctor): How's your recovery going?

B:(Patient): Much better, thanks.

A: Great! Let's schedule a follow-up for next week

B: Sounds good.

A. Any questions or concerns?

B: No, all clear

29.At a Restaurant (Complaint)

A(Customer): I'm sorry, but my food is cold.

B (Waiter): I apologize. Let me get that reheated for you.

A: Thank you.

B: Would you like a complimentary dessert?

A: That's okay, thanks.

B: Sorry once again.

A: No issues please.

30. Introducing Friends

A: Hey, Balu, this is my friend Gopal.

B: Gopal, nice to meet you.!"

A: "Likewise, Balu. I've heard great things about you."

A: "We've been friends since college."

B: "That's awesome. What brings you here tonight?"

A: To attend a Marriage.

31.Apologizing for a Mistake

A: Hey, I'm really sorry...

B: "What are you talking about?"

A: "I forgot to call you back. I feel terrible."

B: "No worries, stuff happens. Let's catch up soon."

A: Shall we meet tomorrow.

B: Sure.

32.Declining an Invitation

A: Hello, do you want to grab dinner tonight?"

B: "Thanks for inviting me, but I have a family gathering."

A: No problem, maybe next time?"

B: Definitely, I 'll surely come.

A: You're most welcome, friend.

B: Thanks a lot.

33.Offering Sympathy.

A: I just lost my grandma. I'm really down.

B: I 'm so sorry to hear that. My condolences.

A: Thanks for listening. It means a lot.

B: Take all the time you need. We 're here for you.

A: It's very kind of you... Thank you.

34.Meeting a New Colleague

A: Hi, I'm Babu. Welcome to the team!

B: Hi, Babu, nice to meet you. I'm excited to start.

A: We're glad to have you, Krishna, Let me show you around.

B: Thanks, I appreciate the help

A: Pleasure is mine...

35.Ending a Conversation

A: It was nice to meet you, but I have to leave shortly.

B: Yeah, me too. Nice running into you

A: Definitely, let's do it again soon.

B: Sounds good. Take care.

A: Sure, you too please

36.Asking for Advice

A: I am having trouble deciding on a major subject in my UG.

B: What are your interests?

 A. I love writing and art

B: Consider creative writing or graphic design. A: Thank you very much for your timely advice

B: Pleasure is mine.

\

37.Giving a Complement

A: Your presentation was amazing today!

B: Thanks. But I was nervous

A: You did great! Your hard work paid off

B: Thanks for the encouragement

A: Pleasure is mine

38.Resolving a Misunderstanding

A: You said you 'd meet me at 7 am.

B: Sorry, shall we catch up now?

A: Okay, no worries, Let's move forward

B: Sorry, Excuse me for my misunderstanding.

39.Saying Goodbye

A: I will miss you, stay in touch,

B: Definitely, thanks for being an amazing friend. Love you!

take care.

A: Very kind of you. Thank you

40.Sharing News

A: I have an exciting news – I 'm getting married!"

B: Congratulations! Thrilled to hear.

A: Thanks, I am really happy.

B: When is the big day

A: Next month 15th.

B: Glad, will attend your marriage for sure.

41.Reminiscence.

A: Remember the last summer vacation at the lake?

B: How could I forget?

A: We should do it again.

B; Definitely, let 's plan something.

A: Shall we go there next week.

B: By all means.

42.Catching Up

A: What 's new with you? Any updates?

B: Just started a new job. How about you?

A: Same old, same old. But happy to see you.

B: Likewise.

A: Let 's have a cup of coffee.

B: Sure. Thanks.

43.Thanking

A: Thanks for hosting dinner tonight.

B: Anytime, happy to have everyone together.

A: You always make us feel welcome.

B: That's what family is for.

A: When should we come to your home?

B: Please come before 7.30 pm.

A: Sure. Thank you.

44.Supporting

A: I'm going through a tough time."

B: I 'm here for you. What do you need?"

A. Thank you.I am in need of a rented house immediately.

B: No worries. Our upstairs portion is vacant only. You can occupy it.

A: Thank you very much for your timely support.

46.Diwali Celebration

A: Hey, happy Diwali! What 's your favourite crackers?

B. I love lighting the diyas, What's your choice?

A: I like firing ground chakras and some big crackers.

B: Good... Do you prepare sweets?

A: Yes, my family makes amazing Gulab jamun.

B: Yum! Do you have a favourite Diwali tradition?

A: Yeah, we exchange gifts and wear new clothes.

B: That sounds wonderful.

45. At a Dinner

A: Pass the mashed potatoes, please.

B: Here you go. How is your day today?

A: Good, a little busy. You?

B. Same. How are your kids?

A: They have grown up fast. Studying in college.

B: Glad to hear

47.Eld-of-Fitr

A: Eid Mubarak! How do you celebrate?

B. We gather with family, exchange gifts, and eat dates.

A That sounds wonderful. What is the significance of Eid?

B: It marks the end of Ramadan, a time of fasting

A: l respect that. Do you have a favourite Eid memory?

B: Yes, praying together in mosques with community.

48.Navratri

A: Happy Navratri Do you dance during Navratri nights?

B: Yes, I love the energy and music.

A: Same here, What's your favourite Dance step.

B: The dandiya is my favourite.

A: That 's so much fun. Do you fast during Navratri?

B: Yes, It's a time for special reflection.

49. Christmas

A: Merry Christmas! What 's your favourite holiday tradition?

B. Decorating the tree and singing carols

A: That sounds magical. Do you have a favourite Christmas memory?

B: Yes, opening gifts with family. That's special.

A: What 's the true meaning of Christmas to you?

B: Giving, love, and kindness.

50. Indian Diwali Sweets.

A: What 's your favourite Diwali sweet?

B: Gulab jamun! My mom's recipe is legendary.

A; Yum! What 's the secret ingredient?

B; Cardamom and rosewater. We fry dumplings and dip them in sugar syrup.

A: Sounds divine. Do you make them together?

B. Yes, It 's a family tradition.

51.Japanese Sushi.

A: Sushi is my favourite Japanese food.

B: Mine too! My daddy takes sushi-making classes.

A: That's great.! What's the most challenging part?

B: Preparing the rice. It needs perfect vinegar balance.

A: I never knew. Do you have a favourite sushi roll?"

B: Spicy tuna, always. I shall share with you.

A: Thanks a million...

Different ways to say 'sorry' during online meeting.

- **I** apologize for that.
- My apologies
- Please excuse me.
- Sorry for the interruption.
- Pardon me for that.
- I regret the mistake.
- I didn't mean to do that sorry.
- I 'm Sorry for the confusion.
- I apologize for the oversight.
- I'm sorry that was unintentional.

Other ways to say "I don't know"

1. I 'm not sure.

2. I 'm uncertain.

3. I don 't have that information.

4. I 'm not aware of that.

5. I 'm unclear on that.

6. I don 't possess that data.

7. I 'm unable to provide an answer.

8. No clue.

9. No idea.

10. I 'm not an expert.

11. That's a good question, but...

12. I 'm not sure, but I can find out.

13. Let me check on that.

14. I 'm not familiar with that, can you explain?"

15.I 'm not sure, what do you think?"

Some common sentences used at a railway station

1. "What time does the next train arrive?"

2. "Which platform is the train departing from?"

3. "Where can I buy a ticket?"

4. "Is this the train to [destination]?"

5. "How much is a ticket to [destination]?"

6. "When will the train leave?"

7. "Can I get a refund for my ticket?"

8. "Is this a direct train, or do I need to change?"

9. "How long is the journey?"

10. "Where can I find the timetable?"

11. "Is the train delayed?"

12. "What time will we reach [destination]?"

13. "Do you have any seats available?"

14. "Can you help me with my luggage?"

15. "Where is the waiting room?"

16. "Is there a restroom nearby?"

17. "Can I reserve a seat in advance?"

18. "Where can I find the nearest exit?"

19. "How do I get to platform [number]?"

20. "Can you tell me the train's final stop?"

Some common sentences used at a bus stand:

1.When is the next bus to [destination]?

2. Which platform is the [bus number] leaving from?

3. Is this bus going to [destination]?

4. How long until the next bus arrives?

5. What time does the last bus leave?

6. One ticket to [destination], please.

7. How much is the fare to [destination]?

8. Can I buy a return ticket?

9. May I board the bus?

10. Excuse me, I need to get off.

11.Where is the bus station/terminal

12.Stop here, please.

13.Can you turn up/down the AC?

14. Is this the express bus?

15.Do you have change for [amount]?

Introducing Yourself.

• Happy morning/AN/Evening__________ sir/ mam

• I am_____ name)

• I am ______years old.

• I live in____________ district, at present

• There are _____ persons in our family.

• I like____________ (fruits' names)

• I am a ______ (Vegetarian/ Non vegetarian)

• I enjoy Watching TV sometimes.

• I am interested in ______________ (Sport's name)

• My hobby is. ___________ (Gardening/ Reading etc)

• My ambition is to become a _________ (doctor/ teacher etc. any one)

Some Tongue Twisters for practice

• Tongue Twisters will improve your pronunciation and fluency.

• Shiena leads, Sheela needs

• If a dog chews shoes, whose shoes does he chew?

• Top chopstick shops stock top chop sticks.

• Selfish, shell fish (repeat several times)

• No need to light a night light on a light night like tonight

• There are thirty thousand feathers on a thrush's throat.

• The great Greek grape growers grow great Greek grapes.

• Linda Lou Lambard loves lemon lollipop lip glass.

• Near a ear, a nearer ear a nearly eerie ear.

• Roberta ran rings around the Roman ruins.

• He threw three free throws.

• A happy hippo hopped and hiccupped.

• Toy boat, toy boat toy boat (repeat)

• A synonym for cinnamon is a cinnamon synonym

• One -one was a race horse, Two - two was one too. One – one won the race. Two-two won the one too.

10.Conclusion

I do hope these simple and easy materials will help the beginners who aspire to start talking in English. As a teacher educator, as a best sorter of information, I have gathered some useful information from some books on communication skills and social media through internet. I express my eternal thanks to those sources which helped to pen-down this booklet. I have slightly modified them to make them easy for the beginners to understand and apply them in their daily life situations.

I request you to make use of these materials to enhance your English vocabulary and the basic skills of the English language and in particular your Speaking skills in English by practising the Dialogues for Conversational practice without fear and shyness consistently.

Your feedback and suggestions are solicited for refining these materials in future.

www.ingramcontent.com/pod-product-compliance
Lightning Source LLC
Chambersburg PA
CBHW040817120726
48005CB00012B/1439